"HOLD ON, *My Child!*"

"HOLD ON, *My Child!*"

A life story of God's All Sufficient Grace

Joy Shields-Miller, MD

XULON PRESS

Xulon Press
2301 Lucien Way #415
Maitland, FL 32751
407.339.4217
www.xulonpress.com

© 2022 by Joy Shields-Miller, MD

All rights reserved solely by the author. The author guarantees all contents are original and do not infringe upon the legal rights of any other person or work. No part of this book may be reproduced in any form without the permission of the author.

Due to the changing nature of the Internet, if there are any web addresses, links, or URLs included in this manuscript, these may have been altered and may no longer be accessible. The views and opinions shared in this book belong solely to the author and do not necessarily reflect those of the publisher. The publisher therefore disclaims responsibility for the views or opinions expressed within the work.

Lyric quotations taken from Johnson Oatman Jr., "Higher Ground," *public domain.*

Lyric quotations taken from The Gaithers, "Joy Comes in the Morning," Copyright © by Capitol CMG Publishing, Non-commercial License No. 1020079 (executed November 3, 2021).

Unless otherwise indicated, Scripture quotations taken from the King James Version (KJV)–*public domain.*

Paperback ISBN-13: 978-1-66283-754-8
Ebook ISBN-13: 978-1-66283-755-5

Dedication

This is Grandma Joy's Story —
Dedicated to our grandchildren Kate, Anna, Camden, Jagger, and Palmer. May you all always follow Jesus throughout your lives!

Foreword

By
David E. Miller, Ph.D.,
Husband & Best Friend

To know Joy Shields, MD (aka Dr. Joy Shields-Miller), is to love her! Her radiant smile is contagious as she practices kindness to all, giving everyone the benefit of the doubt, and allowing her life to be a genuine reflection of Christ's love for mankind. However, behind the smile and the love she reflects so remarkably well, there is a side to her life that very few know. Only a few trusted friends and family have heard her story and can begin to understand the momentous obstacles and challenges she had to overcome since the very early years of her life.

As her husband and best friend, I have marveled at the manner in which she has allowed God to provide the ALL SUFFICIENT GRACE described in II Corinthians 12:9, not just occasionally when most folk experience a need for God's touch—but literally every day of her life. Despite multiple surgeries that have provided some improvements, she has had daily medical challenges since childhood and likely will have these until she reaches her Heavenly home where she will have complete healing and a perfect body. In addition to the medical issues, Joy sustained substantial emotional deficits and at times was the victim of severe emotional abuse.

In January 2021, I encouraged Joy to think about writing her story; something I had used multiple times with my patients who needed resolution of deep hurts or unresolved conflicts from their past. I also desired that our children and five grandchildren know her story; what God faithfully had helped her overcome. I wanted them to hear how their Grandma Joy had overcome such mammoth crises in this life through trusting God and relying upon His promises.

At first, Joy was reluctant to agree to this project, for it meant re-visiting some very painful memories that time had helped to distance from her mind. Furthermore, she worried that others might question her motive; she feared some might conclude it to be an attack or retribution toward her mother. But true to her faithfulness to God, she prayerfully considered what God would desire of her, and decided to write her story. This exercise brought much healing and helped Joy tremendously; it reversed those occasional doubts experienced and validated in her mind that she had in fact sincerely forgiven her offenders.

Foreword

The first version of this story was written on a WORD document with some early pictures inserted throughout the narrative. It was only shared with a very few close friends with a disclaimer to not share beyond their reading or place on social media in any way. Joy desired to prevent her story from reaching her mother since the details of her mother's relationship with her might hurt her mother. With the recent passing of Joy's mom in October 2021, several of our most trusted friends encouraged Joy to proceed with publishing this book.

Table of Contents

Chapter 1: My Beginning Years............1
Chapter 2: Early Medical & Health Issues.........9
Chapter 3: Dysfunctional Home Life...........13
Chapter 4: Challenging Parent-Child Relationships...................17
Chapter 5: Christian Heritage............21
Chapter 6: God's Amazing Grace.............27
Chapter 7: First Marriage & Early Adult Years.....31
Chapter 8: A Precious Friend's Loyalty..........35
Chapter 9: Marriage Failure 43
Chapter 10: Multiple Surgeries & Treatments.................49
Chapter 11: My Testimony..................57
Chapter 12: God's Enabling Grace............65
Chapter 13: God Brought Surgical Healing to the Surgeon............67
Chapter 14: Final Years of Practice.............71
Chapter 15: A Multitude of Positive Influences Along the Way..........77

Chapter 1
My Beginning Years

I was born February 9th, in 1961. My parents had been married 10 years trying to have kids. They loved kids. They had 3 miscarriages over the 10 year period and then my older sister, Kathy, was born, but with a collapsed lung. 26 months later I was born with spina bifida and had an orange-sized tumor to the right side of my spine. My parents were afraid that another child might be even more severely disabled so they decided not to have any more kids. Mom unfortunately developed a uterine abscess after my birth, and underwent a hysterectomy. I think she overall felt that to be my fault. They really weren't ready to stop having kids. Someone had to be blamed and Mom frequently reminded me of the trauma I caused her during my birth.

At 13 months, I had my first surgery to try to remove the tumor. I would not, or could not, let my feet touch the floor or bear weight. I couldn't even crawl. I scooted. The surgery did not help. At age 2, my parents took me to a small chapel at the end of a revival service, where Rev. A.B. Maloy, Jr. was preaching, who would later become our pastor when my parents decided to attend his church. The invitation to pray had been given and church was dismissed, but they carried me up front and placed me on the altar where I was anointed and prayed over. Three days later, for the first time, I pulled myself up to my feet and walked.

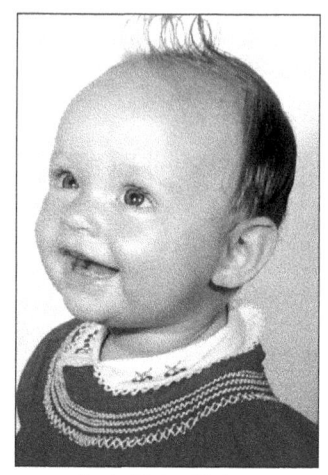

Joy's Baby Picture

I can remember my Mom saying that I was always too busy to go to the bathroom and didn't care if my diaper was full. Actually, I could not feel that I had done anything as bowel and bladder control were still compromised. I don't know why God would heal me enough to not be paralyzed, yet allow a life-long battle with compromise directly from the spina bifida to

Kathy (left) with sister Joy (right)

continue. But, He had a plan for me as I will develop further in my story.

My sister and I were reportedly close at ages 4 and 2 respectively, loved farm animals, especially horses and played like she was James Drury, "The Virginian" on TV, and I was Randy, a cowhand, on that same show. We played together for hours and hours with small metal farm trucks, horse trailers, plastic cattle, and horses. We each had a measurable distaste for dolls. We would both likely be seen as "tomboys." Then my sister got sick, very sick. Diagnosed with leukemia, she suffered for 20 months receiving the harshest chemo, the only chemo available at the time. Kathy died two days after her 7th birthday, I was only 4 ½.

I remember Dad carrying me back home from grandma and grandpa's (who lived next door to us) the night Kathy passed away at the hospital. Mom carried her 2 iron skillets that grandma had borrowed and I, with arms around my Daddy's neck looked up into a pitch black night sky not quite sure why there was such a heavy blanketed sadness on everybody.

I begged my parents to let me go see Kathy at the

Kathy (left) and Joy (right)

funeral home, during visiting hours. I promised I would not cry. They did, but regretted it later. I walked up to her casket, held on to the edge, and kept telling her to come on and get up, to wake up and play with me. Tears were streaming down my face and I accidentally made smudge marks on the velvet overlay. I was always blamed for that too. Others paying respects were all moved to tears, not a dry eye present.

Joy (left) and Kathy (right)

Following this, my Dad went into depression, withdrew, and suffered severe mental anguish that I could not understand. I just wanted him to keep playing with me and taking me rides in the wagon. But, he couldn't. Mom told me years later that Dad had asked Kathy's doctor if they could take my father's blood and give it to Kathy while giving hers to him so that he would die and she would live. Still, it was easier to live with Dad in my elementary years than Mom. My mother had 3 nervous breakdowns during this time and turned to prescription drug abuse. She was unpredictable. Her yelling and screaming, sometimes throughout the house, were traumatizing. It happened every day after Dad got home from work at 4:00 PM. We had no air conditioning so the windows were all open. In a small, close neighborhood, I would be so embarrassed because Mom's yelling could be heard by many, many people through their own open windows or if they were walking down our street.

I remember her telling me once to stop playing with broken glass when I was just holding a necklace. She frequently threatened suicide to get my Dad's attention while he remained silent. No doubt Mom thought he didn't care about her. Mom's actions precipitated into hallucinations of seeing faces in the walls as she became more and more paranoid. Talk about scary! Her eyes would get huge as she stomped through the house and her words sometimes slurred at night. Many times I awoke to her falling in the bathroom and not being able to get up. I had to help her. Dad continued to withdraw. Mom once whispered to me, as I was crying and begging her not to commit suicide, that she was just doing it to get my Dad's attention – she would not really kill herself. What a relief! I had been in agony thinking my Mom was going to go to hell and would never get to see Kathy, my sister, again.

Mom frequently would became loud and violent. She would use a fly swatter or tree branch for punishment and was quick to assume I had done something wrong. She even blamed me for multiple things I never did. My Pastor, Rev. A.B. Maloy, Jr., confided in me later, my mom blamed me for things that Kathy had actually done like running through his home looking in drawers when we visited while I just played for 2 hours by myself in his living room. Kathy became angelic to Mom and whenever I did or said a minor infraction, I was told that Kathy would not have behaved in that manner.

Mom also had a special concoction to induce emesis whenever she thought I had eaten or drunk something poisonous. Believe me, syrup of ipecac would not hold a candle to this regimen composed of raw eggs, mustard, warm water, and, I think vinegar. This was administered when I chewed up four orange flavored baby aspirin, once when she said I drank a bottle of turpentine (hard to believe a kid would even taste it), and again when I reported that my friend and I ate some wild honeysuckle droplets. My friend did not drop over dead; nor did her mom make her throw up. I learned not to report everything I had to eat or drink.

Rev. A.B. Maloy, Jr.

I cried a lot and had multiple episodes of wetting myself as I could not contain control under such stress. Mom later told me that all they would have to do is look at me sternly and I would break into tears. She sometimes looked at me that way just to see if I would cry. I always did! Some embarrassing moments for me are included in the following chapters.

Chapter 2
EARLY MEDICAL & HEALTH ISSUES

In first grade I had to sit on the edge of my chair to not have accidents and one time it failed, I had pee leak out onto the floor. I got up to get paper towels to clean it up and was mortified that my teacher loudly asked in front of the class what had happened. I tried desperately to save face and not lie so I told her that someone had spilled some water and I was going to clean it up. Now, I would hope that most teachers would let an accident of this nature go and address in private, but not my teacher…she must have felt that it would

Joy during elementary years

be better to use me as an example to the class by stating loudly that all someone has to do to go to the bathroom is to hold up their hand.

One time I soaked a saddle and was concerned it might never recover although thoroughly washed with soap and water. When playing softball I would either have to not drink anything for 3 or 4 hours, or, when I started using a catheter, take it with me to ballfields where there was no bathroom and use it inside the car into a bottle… no easy task. Using the catheter started when I was 19 as my spinal cord was tethered. The lower spine itself actually never developed but branched out like an upside down wishbone. I had no tailbone, just cartilage and skin over the cauda equina (mass of nerves) at the base of my spine. Frequent urinary tract infections became common for me. At age 19, I had to have my urethra dilated to remove the infection and was on oral antibiotics for long periods of time. Common to those medications, I continuously felt nauseated and fatigued.

In my third year of medical school, when on call during a strenuous surgery rotation, I became so sick that I dropped out for 3 months. By the time I was an OB/GYN resident, I was hurrying to the bathroom about 5 to 7 times a day changing pads and getting cleaned up to go back to work. I did not disclose my handicap during my two years of Family Practice Residency or during my OB/GYN Residency because I didn't want fellow residents to feel like they had to give me special treatment, or worse, be resentful thinking I wasn't holding up my fair end of the work. Only in my last few months did I share my condition with another OB senior resident, Clara Regal, MD. She couldn't fathom how someone could cope with this condition while dealing with the stress characterized by residency. She told me that I just became her new hero.

I shared my condition with only one other person while in OB/GYN training—Dr. Robert A. Welch, senior perinatologist. Dr. Welch, a genuine mentor to me, became Residency Director of our program after I graduated. He told me that there would not be a judge in the entire land that would not grant me disability if I requested it. I did not wish to do that. Thank God, I never had to.

Only God could have provided the stamina to keep going. I trusted in Him and that I was accomplishing His Will for my life. Someone once said that if I had not had this conviction, I might have quit. I prayed daily, throughout the day, and did my best to live for Him and be a Christian witness to those He directed my way.

Chapter 3
DYSFUNCTIONAL HOME LIFE

In my early years at home, we were too poor to have a horse and the pony that was actually given to my sister when she was sick, had to be sold after she died. Our family cat left one week after Kathy died. In a short time period, I lost my sister, pony, and cat. Maybe that is why I cling to animals as an adult needing to keep a horse, dog, and outside barn cats at our home.

Joy with pet pony Zippy

A few kids lived near me, but Mom was overly protective – perhaps fearful of further loss in her life. She wouldn't let me go to camp or have friends over for more than an hour at a time. I had only one birthday party in which I could invite over friends at age 8. Mom believed birthday and graduation parties were just a way for people to "bum gifts" off other people and so those events were essentially forbidden. I was desperately lonely and remember kneeling on the sofa watching the rain outside the large glass window while I cried. I received a $2 weekly allowance for dusting everything in the house. Everything had to be removed from all the furniture, dusted and put back in place after the furniture holding the articles was thoroughly cleaned including the sides and back if possible. I hate dusting to this day. Our kids and grandkids do not buy Grandma any "dust collectors."

I also received $1 for every "A" on my grade card and these monies, from dusting and "A"s, I saved to go to college since Mom clearly indicated she had no intention of helping with my education. When Dad was partially laid off work once, I found out my Mom reduced the usual 10% tithe we contributed to our church to half the amount. I was also dismayed when I discovered she didn't pay any tithe on odd jobs that produced supplemental income. This discovery worried me greatly since I had learned we were supposed to tithe our income. In my childish mind, I figured that if I made up the difference, maybe my Mom and Dad would not be held accountable by God, and could still make it to Heaven. Once I gave $185 of my savings, and another time, I gave $150, without either of them ever knowing. I knew they would be upset so I never told them.

The money I saved never got used for college. Our old car needed so many repairs that we had to replace it with a new one when I was 14 or 15 years old. I offered the rest of my money, $400, to help them get the new family car. They didn't want to take it but I convinced them the car would be used for things I needed too, and, therefore I wanted to share a part of making it happen. My own first car could not be bought until I was 20 years old. It was a cherry red slant 6 Dodge Dart Swinger, and it was immaculate and beautiful! I needed it to drive back and forth from OSU to home on weekends as I wanted to continue going to my home church whenever possible.

Another memory of college days, that seems impossible even now, was during one of my trips back to OSU I noticed my gas gauge went down to empty. I pulled into a parking lot and called Mom & Dad. Responding to my urgent need, they brought me a gas can full of gas, but my car didn't need it. Remarkably, we watched the gauge spontaneously climb back up to full by itself after they arrived. While waiting on them I began making good use of my time studying chemistry. It spoke to my Dad's heart how that my trust in God in all situations could lead to enough peace in my heart to actually be studying instead of worrying. I explained that I undoubtedly believed that

God allowed that to happen for a reason to protect me… that maybe if I had continued on, I would have been involved in an accident.

Chapter 4
CHALLENGING PARENT-CHILD RELATIONSHIPS

I absolutely loved to play softball at school and loved to be around horses any chance I could get. Of course, I had to have ready access to bathrooms whatever I did. My uncle Dave, who was 13 years older than me and played on a church softball team was my savior at the time. He could drive me to ball practices and games and bought a reddish-brown and white pinto pony for me for $35 when I was 12. We kept her in our back yard for the summer but I had to sell her in the fall since we had no barn. It became a routine of mine to get a horse, any horse, for the summer and then suffer another loss in the fall by selling it. I determined that when I became an adult, and as soon as I had enough money to keep a horse, that I would have one continuously, year in and year out, in my back yard.

"HOLD ON, *My Child!*"

Dad and I became extremely close in my teenage years. Mom frustrated us by initially going with us to special functions, and then insisting on leaving early. Once we went for a day to Kings Island. Dad promised I could stay that day as long as I wanted, which to me was through the fireworks at 10 PM. After all, we went on "vacation" for just **one** day each year! Mom argued to leave at 2 PM. It was a mess. Dad put his foot down, Mom went to the car, and we continued to ride rides. Dad and I rode the roller coaster 6 times in a row.

Once Mom made me leave early during a party with neighbor kids where I spent time picking blackberries and selling them to people for 50 cents a quart to help fund the Pepsi and chips for the party. We were a block away at a home waiting for neighborhood kids who came an hour late. So, 7 minutes into the official party, Mom yelled for me to come home to get my hair washed. She could easily be heard yelling at least a block away. I begged and cried for her to let me stay a little longer but she refused. Everyone else was privileged to eat most of the chips and Pepsi that I had bought for the party. This same thing happened at the only girls' slumber party that I was ever allowed to attend. It started on a Friday night. We went to bed about 4 AM, Mom came to get me at 7 AM! I had to go with her although the parents at that home offered to bring me home later after the other girls got up, had fresh donuts, and got ready to go later in the day. I couldn't even say good-bye since my friends were all still sleeping. Mom said she just figured I would be ready to come home so she came to get me. How I would have loved to stay the whole Saturday!

Mom's excuses to leave early became so frequent, including church events, that Dad and I started discouraging Mom from going with us to any function. Mom began saying that I did not obey my father and mother as the Bible stated. She left the Bible open to that verse and said that I might as well tear it out of the Bible because I didn't do it anyway. She also told me that I was a hypocrite and threatened to say it at church sometime - in front of everyone. Once she got so mad that she tried to strike me in the face. I reflexively grabbed her arm and held her still until the fury subsided. It wasn't until that point that I realized I was stronger than mom and that I could stop her from hitting me. She too came to that conclusion, so she never tried to strike me again.

Late in Mom's life, she had to undergo open heart surgery and have frequent heart catheterizations. It was while I was at her bedside following one such procedure that my childhood came up and I was able to share all the things that she had said or done to me that hurt me the worst. She replied that she didn't remember saying any of the hurtful things, but that she wouldn't deny it either. It was a healing moment for us. I was able to completely forgive her.

When a doctor put her on Neurontin for her nerve pain at the age of 86, she became much easier to be with and less unpredictable. She kept a fully loaded six-gun revolver hidden in her bedroom closet. So, although still on guard, we felt <u>less</u> threatened that she might shoot us. She began accepting our gifts and did not shout that she was going to take us to court for matters of disagreement anymore. My husband shared with me that this medicine is also used for treatment of Bipolar illness; he was fairly certain her behaviors suggested she suffered from Bipolar Disorder. We never told her of the multiple uses for Neurontin; we simply affirmed that her doctor was treating her nerve pain and it was working. How I wish she had been prescribed that about 50 years earlier!

Chapter 5
CHRISTIAN HERITAGE

I already wrote about my first miracle which gave me the ability to walk. My parents were initially very loyal about going to church and taking us kids to be involved in Sunday School, events, fellowships, dinners, etc.

Family Picture: Kathy (left), Mom, Dad, and Joy (right)

At least until I was pre-teen, when my Mom quit going to most services. She would still attend Sunday School and church most weeks on Sunday mornings, but Dad and I absolutely loved going to church. We would be there every time the doors opened, twice on Sunday, Wednesday night prayer and praise meetings, and even on Saturday nights when we started having prayer meetings at 8:00

PM for the next day's services. Revivals at our church could go on for weeks and Dad and I attended faithfully every night.

When I was 4 years old, just after my sister Kathy died, following a Billy Graham crusade service on a Monday night TV station, I asked Mom if I could pray to ask God into my heart. I did it as best as I knew how while kneeling in front of our living room couch. At 5 years of age, I announced that I was going to be a foreign missionary. They had only one child now, so this was not met with exuberating joy by my parents who tried to discourage me in many ways for years and years. During my freshman year at Circleville Bible College, I asked about going to Kenya, Africa in between my 1st and 2nd year. I was told that I wasn't old enough, but I completed an application anyway, prayed about it, then left it with God to work out the details. I figured God would either provide a means or close the option. God didn't close the option; in fact, I was accepted for a 6 1/2 week term. I totally left it up to God to provide the money; my family was poor and couldn't raise the funds needed for this experience. I was invited to speak at 4 different churches in order to raise the needed funding for my trip. After hearing of my proposed short-term mission trip, each church would take up a love offering to help me out with expenses.

My Dad, who was on a strict $20 per week allowance from my Mom, mostly used to buy gas to go back and forth to work, saved enough back somehow to give me $100. This was surprising since Dad had not wanted me to go and later told me how he was praying that if I went, I wouldn't be able to tolerate the weather and so never go back. I later discovered that my Dad would forego a can of Coke during his afternoon break from his job as a laborer at a brick yard, so he could save 50 cents per day to be able to give me. He worked in an open air kiln much of the time. Even in the hottest of summer days, he sacrificed this simple refreshing cold treat during his break, in order to save up enough money to then present me with a $100 bill, which he did several times during my college days as well.

My 6 week trip to Kenya was awesome. It was while there, at Tenwek Hospital, that I met Billy Graham's son, Franklin, and where I felt God calling me to be a surgeon. Knowing what the next 10 years of my life would hold, as far as education goes, was a relief. I remember being told that my mom had called to talk to Dr. Dan Tipton, our General Superintendent then, prior to me leaving for Kenya to tell him that God had told her if I go, that she would not be alive when I returned. Obviously, God did not tell her that.

My Mom had told me repeatedly that I would never go even one year to college as they could not afford it. I fervently prayed for God's Will to be done and I told God that I would do all that I could do to get to college if He would provide the funds. I went another year to Circleville Bible College, took more courses on missions, then transferred to Ohio State University to get a BA in chemistry so that I could apply for medical school. I had completely dedicated my life to God at age 15; I desired that God be in total control of my life, career, and my entire future. This total surrendering to God's Will is what our church doctrine describes as "sanctification."

Once I figured out what God wanted me to do, it seemed I could trust Him for the funds to do it. If the money didn't come, I would believe that it wasn't the right timing or that God had something else in mind. You see, I must have prayed 100,000 times to be saved between the ages of 4 and 15 just in case I didn't do it right at age 4. I loved my pastor, but he was all about hellfire and brimstone and coming up short as a Christian, the Judgments, etc. At times I went to the altar at church on a habitual basis for fear I had jeopardized my relationship with God by being grouchy at my parents. I never went into deep sin. I would have been scared to death that God would send me to hell before I repented! Now, in a way, that was good – I never drank alcohol, never smoked, never used drugs, never had sex until my wedding night, etc.

Later, I discovered that my obsessive worries were a part of a diagnosis of OCD or obsessive compulsive disorder. My loving husband, a Christian psychologist, helped me tremendously with this after we married in

1999. Reading and working through a book on religious scrupulosity was eye-opening. I still struggle with these thoughts at times, but not constantly. Medication helps.

As stated earlier, I knew I could pray to God and that He would get me through college if it was His Will that I go. I filled out every application, retrieved every reference, and did all the leg work that I could to get scholarships and grants. This effort took hours and hours. Money for the needed amounts came in from unpredictable sources. For the first 4 years of my college life, this came in semester by semester sometimes at what seemed like the last possible moment. Once a check came in signed by a bank executive to keep the donor anonymous to me. I remember praying to God that it would be so much easier on me if I didn't have to worry from semester to semester about whether the money would be available to continue my training. God did not chide me about this lack of complete and total trust, but He took care of it. It was discovered right before my last 2 years at the Ohio State University (OSU) that due to my spinal cord birth defect, the Bureau of Vocational Rehabilitation would cover my room, board, and books. I was able to get through Bible College for 2 years and obtain my pre-med degree, 5 total years of college, without any debt!

God answered many prayer requests I had prior to and during attendance at OSU. He provided the money, my Dodge Dart Swinger which only had 60,000 miles for only $1200, a Christian roommate in an all girls' dorm, a wonderful job for work-study in a microbiology lab that I loved, a parking garage spot right across the road from my dorm when I was told it might be several miles away and that I would have to get back to my dorm by shuttle. The parking garage, although close, was kind of a scary place to be. I would sing "Amazing Grace" or "There is Power in the Blood" while walking out of it to and from my dorm. I also carried my Bible on top of all my books. I felt this would cause most would-be assailants to at least take pause. A girlfriend of mine shared that two guys who later came to Christ via Campus Crusade, actually told her that they saw me walking once, considered doing harm to me, but then noticed 2 men, dressed all in white, each about 10 feet tall, walking beside me on either side. Wow! Her report of this gives me chills to this day.

Joy and her Dad at Medical College graduation

Chapter 6
GOD'S AMAZING GRACE

I lacked physical stamina after age 19, to do many things that I would have loved to do, like play softball. My limitations were worsening with age until I was wearing a catheter attached to a leg bag while performing surgeries at age 35. However, God provided me with increased ability in reading and memorization during earlier years. No one may believe this, but I began reading at age 2 ½. I would sit on my pediatric neurosurgeon's leg at the age of 3 and read the newspaper to him. Memorization was easy and fun. I won 3 spelling bee championships from 6th to 8th grade. I also participated in Bible Quizzing, leading our team to a regional championship. At age 17, I could quote full passages of Scripture for 1 ½ hours straight. I memorized, word for word in the King James Version, the book of Philippians. I wanted to memorize a book of the Bible and chose Philippians because it was about joy.

"HOLD ON, My Child!"

I could win against many pastors and evangelists on questions about biblical contents, names, places, etc., in just about every game. To this day, no one will play Bible Scattergories or other games similar to that with me because they figure I would win. Little do they know that I am not nearly as clear minded at age 60 as I was back in my teen and young adult years; and, it is getting more difficult to call to mind exact verses and matching references. That's ok because God knows I don't need to master memorization now like I did back then.

This God-given ability helped me, with intense study on my part by spending hours at my desk instead of socializing, to make straight "A"s in high school and be valedictorian of my class. I transferred from Bible College to the Ohio State University with a 3.95 GPA and, graduated with a BA in chemistry at OSU with, as I recall, a 3.86 GPA after taking some of the most difficult classes offered. Some of my classes were post-graduate

Joy and high school Chemistry teacher Mr. Bowman

work. These successes qualified me for entrance into Medical School.

Prior to that, and while at Circleville Bible College, I met and dated a young man whom I would have married had he asked, but he told me that he could not date a doctor since he felt God had forbidden him to continue dating a nurse. I still cannot figure that one out. This gentleman also said that God had called him to the mission field, but he had told God no. I believed that he would give in to God's call on his life and things would work out. They didn't; so we went separate ways.

This break-up left me so heartbroken that I did not even date for 3 years. I am a very loyal person--probably to a fault. However, this allowed me to concentrate on difficult subjects that required a lot of time for study. During this time, there was a song that seemed to inspire me to keep going. The song was entitled "Higher Ground" and was written in 1892 by Johnson Oatman Jr. and Charles H. Gabriel. I cherished the words of this song so much that I typed them out and kept them taped to my desk. The lyrics follow:

Verses:
I'm pressing on the up-ward way. New heights I'm gaining every day;
Still praying as I on-ward bound, "Lord, plant my feet on higher ground"

My heart has no desire to stay, Where doubts arise and fears dismay.
Tho' some may dwell where these abound, My prayer, my aim, is higher ground

I want to live above the world, Tho' Satan's darts at me are hurled;
For faith has caught the joyful sound, The song of saints on higher ground

I want to scale the utmost height, And catch a gleam of glory bright;
But still I'll pray till heav'n I've found, "Lord, lead me on to higher ground"

Chorus
Lord, lift me up and let me stand, By faith, on heaven's table land,
A higher plane than I have found. Lord, plant my feet on higher ground.

Chapter 7
First Marriage & Early Adult Years

In 1983, a chemistry teaching assistant began to show attention to me. He was funny and kind. We enjoyed being with each other. He didn't seem to mind my strict Christian values or listening to Christian music in my dorm room – the only music I listened to. I had always been taught to only date a Christian. So, initially, we didn't officially date – just met at McDonalds maybe, or he walked me back to my dorm, or he showed me where he worked. I did share Christ with him a lot. One Monday, he let me know that he had asked Christ into his heart. I was thrilled! We started going to church together. He struggled with alcohol and I tried to help and encourage. He also had had some intimate previous relationships, but I forgave him. And, when I discovered a closet full of beer cans and some pornographic pictures while he was cleaning out a closet in his apartment, I was horrified but naively kept trying to believe he was ending this lifestyle.

I rationalized at the time that he was, after all, getting rid of the sin. I should have talked with a spiritual leader, but didn't. I figured no one would understand how committed he was to living a Godly life and that they would just judge him for his past. When he asked me to marry him, I remember praying and praying that it would be okay by God for us to get married. I can now clearly see my decision making was seriously compromised by my desperation to avoid going back to a dysfunctional home.

I couldn't go home that summer because Mom had thrown Dad out, left him a pair of shoes and a change of clothes on the back porch, and changed the locks. I was actually afraid to go back to live with Mom for the summer and Dad was displaced trying to find his way and get a permanent place to live. I was afraid to live with Mom and afraid of what she might do if I went to live with Dad. Mom was abusive at times; she once threatened my Dad with a gun to his head and dared him to move. He didn't move, but replied for her to go ahead and shoot, that he would be better off. Now, this may sound comical, but it was seriously traumatizing for me. Another time Mom came at Dad with an aerosol can to beat him in the head as he was sitting in a rocking chair, but I threw myself over him so that if she proceeded, it would be me that she would hit and not him.

Mom also once told me that she visited my sister's grave, laid down prone on it in the rain, and cried that it was Kathy and not me who had died. Once she dumped onto the porch some Mother's Day flowers I had tried to give to her but couldn't get in as she had locked me out. There was a note that she would not continue to take care of my dog, Princess, any more. In desperation, I drove Princess to my pastor's home where they kept her at their farm. Then, I decided it would be better for me to just go back to my college dorm earlier than planned.

In sharing these events about Mom with Dr. Norman & Nancy Wilson over a meal at the Spaghetti Warehouse, Dr. Norman asked me if my Mom ever went to church. I immediately quipped what Mom would have said had she been there – that she was saved and sanctified! Without missing a beat, Dr. Norman replied, "Ooooh! Well, just imagine what she would have been like had she _not_ been saved and sanctified!" It was great comic relief for the situation.

When talking about my growing up years to my first OB/GYN partner, Dr. Ed Ricaurte, he told me that he knew a young man with an almost identical life growing up who committed suicide at age 18. Dr. Ricaurte marveled that I had made it and asked how. Without hesitation I exclaimed that I only made it because of God! Despite everything dysfunctional about my home life and a poor decision for escaping that home and entering into a marriage that was doomed for failure from the start, God's grace and love for me provided the strength I needed to survive! Although thinking about suicide in times of desperation, God's love for me and my dedication to Him kept me from yielding to any of those self-destructive thoughts.

Chapter 8

A PRECIOUS FRIEND'S LOYALTY

My life story would not be complete without telling about how God brought a most dear and trusted friend to my life, ironically with the same name as my sister who had passed away with leukemia, Kathy. We attended the same church but were on rival town football teams. We loved to go to ballgames together with her home town logo on her jacket and with mine on my jacket. We were a pair! We dressed up as the Lone Ranger and Tonto one year at Bible College. Our very best memories are about going to Nipgen Camp as youth counselors starting at age 15 for me. We would be together at these camps for a whole month each summer. It was an escape from home for me and we could share everything together. We then went to Bible College together and loved being roommates. We were inseparable and everyone knew it.

The Dean of Students, Rev. David Van Hoose, once told us that many peers were actually jealous of our close friendship and wished they could have the same. Kathy has always been a champion for me and can even now be counted on for support.

Best friend Kathy (Tonto) and Joy (Lone Ranger)

While teenagers, we would simply give a distress call over the phone and we knew to meet at our special spot for a conference – the empty parking lot of a food store. We sorted out many things there, it was our safe space. I remember one time my Mom called Kathy to tell her to stay away from me - that Kathy was a bad influence. I was aghast! A sister-in-Christ is a blessing, certainly not ever a bad influence! So ridiculous! I was afraid it would divide us, but Kathy stayed by my side, and at the parking lot, we figured out how we could spend more time together…like going to Nipgen camp as counselors every chance possible. My Dad always supported my trips to camp and Mom lost, despite her dramatically opposing it. Kathy and I would ask for adjoining dorm rooms at camp, get all our little girls to bed and to sleep, then sit outside our doors on the sidewalk eating cheese puffs and drinking Mello Yello while musing over the difficult things in life. We could talk to our camp coordinators as they came by on night rounds.

Many times, Kathy would say something that got me laughing so hard that I needed to race to the bathroom before I lost control. One example was when an evangelist heard us talking about someone we knew named Zula. This preacher only heard the word Zula, so in his southern drawl asked very definitively, "What is a Zula?" It made us hysterical, no time for me to run to a bathroom since a bladder spasm occurred immediately, so I collapsed on my knees onto the sidewalk holding my stomach trying to maintain control while laughing until we both cried. Kathy knew what was happening and forever after only had to say the word, "Zula", for us to start laughing again. This happened more times than I can count and continued into our Bible College years, yet we laughed about it every time.

I had frequent bouts of strep-throat as a child, every winter was a challenge. When at Bible College, bronchitis became the issue and once it was so bad, likely double pneumonia, that I was hospitalized. After 5 days of IV antibiotics and aerosol treatments, I was feeling better and about to be discharged to go back to college. I was walking in the hall of the hospital and stopped to visit with a sweet lady there who became friends with

Kathy and me. She invited us to her and her husband's home in Logan Elm Village. One night we decided to pop in and visit.

Logan Elm Village is a nightmare for trying to locate a residence. Every road branches off into several other roads, but eventually, it seems like they all end in a cul-de-sac. We discovered this one night when a guy yelled at us and jumped into his car to chase us all over the area because we pulled a prank on his neighbor, our music professor, Glenna Brown. We toilet papered her house, we only did that to people we loved although that sounds weird to most. No GPS or even a map back then. We got lost searching for our friends, the Hanenkrat's. I spotted a police car in a driveway and exclaimed that since a policeman lived at that home, it would be safe, and he certainly would know how to get to Tom & Dorothy Hanenkrat's home. We stopped, both of us went to the door. The lady seemed a little nervous. They didn't know the Hanenkrat's so we went on.

Finally we found our new friends and they welcomed us into their home and ordered pizza. When the husband, Tom, came down to the family room after a knock at their door, he brought not only a pizza but a patrolman! It was explained to us that a robbery had occurred at the house where we had stopped to ask directions, and the lady described 3 people – a guy and two girls, one with long brown hair and one with long black hair. Sounded just like us except for the guy! We answered the policeman's questions, begged him not to call our parents (which would worry them to death), and then he told us that although he didn't think a car with a Bible College sticker on the bumper was likely to hold criminals, we were nonetheless, his two prime and _only_ suspects.

What a way to make a first impression on this couple at their home! The pizza got cold as we ate it in shock. Later they became such good friends as we tried to win them to the Lord, that they offered to give us free boarding if we would come to live with them. They told us that we reminded them of their two daughters now miles and miles away. They took us to Godfather's for the best pizza I had ever had. Nothing further ever became of the robbery investigation. We declined to move in with them because the wife, with chronic kidney illness, would be back in the hospital many more times before we eventually lost touch.

Kathy could always make me laugh, even during the worst times in our lives. We watched the same Don Knotts' comedies so often that we could quote the funniest parts and laugh hysterically until we cried, over and over again. Our favorite food at the Bible College was leftover pepperoni and mushroom pizza, cold for breakfast, with a Mello Yello. We felt that was fine dining for us! God blessed and loved our friendship! One time a couple from another town asked us to house-sit for them while they were away on vacation. We didn't have any spare money for gas to do this and the Sunday night immediately before this could even be a possibility, a gentleman, Harry Thacker, from our church called us over and said, "God told me to give $20 to each of you, <u>and told me to tell you to just go and have fun with it</u>!" Harry was a Sunday School teacher. Wow! It stamped an indelible impression on our young minds that GOD would care about us so much that He spoke to this man about it; and, that God would <u>specify</u> that we have a good time with the money provided for our stay!

Another time related to money was when Kathy asked me to go in with her to take out a half share on a missionary couple per month. I didn't think I could do it, but silently vowed to God that if He provided this money every month, I would give it. He never failed including the one month that was almost to pass by when I came upon enough money, laying on a sidewalk in front of me, to cover not only that month but 80% of the next month's amount. I remember looking up at the sky through beautiful tree leaves and feeling God's blessing all over me. Kathy and I once again could marvel at how intimately God knew us and how He provided even little detailed things.

We were both involved in work-study programs at the college. She helped out in the library and I washed dishes in the cafeteria. That was my first job. I remember being so excited when the boss promoted me to Captain of the dishwashing team that I used the payphone to call home about it! The next year I became Dean of Student's secretary. No way I could type close to the words per minute of the girl before me. She rattled through the keys to produce 90 words a minute; I could only do 51 at best with one mistake. No one ever knew, except Kathy, that I came back almost every night, and on Saturdays on my own time to complete the work that I felt should have been done during the weekdays if only I was better at typing. I loved that office and took great care to keep it spotless and dignified. The housekeeping person was not up to par for my standards and, although I despised dusting, I polished the furniture for a continual shine.

Kathy was there for me during difficult childhood years, difficult teen years, and certainly during my difficult first marriage. It was she who listened for hours as I languished over the phone and told me, "You don't deserve this." It was so impactful and healing at the time.

Chapter 9
Marriage Failure

I was trying to figure out where I went wrong in a marriage where my husband was clandestinely, in our very first year of marriage, still writing to a former girlfriend that he had been intimate with just prior to knowing me, when she lived many states away; how he quietly got involved with someone in cocaine anonymous and had this lady's kids' toys in a locked detached garage; why there was a note on my kitchen door one day that if he didn't pay the money owed this person, that she would tell the school where he taught, and me, everything. Also, I found, to my utter horror and dismay, pornographic videos and multiple beer cans in a second bedroom. Most of this happened when we were living separately due to where my residency had placed me and these 'discoveries' were made when I could come home for a weekend.

Once I discovered an unplayed voice mail from another woman, married, who was lamenting that they had missed their routine Tuesday lunch together. All of these incidents, and others, were confronted, but I was always given an excuse like, "I was trying to help that person come to know the Lord," or, "I wanted to be a witness to them," or, "I was just helping out since AA helped me in the past." And, then came the blame. He would attack me by saying if I was truly a Christian and had forgiven him for his past, I wouldn't be asking accountability questions, that if I was really saved and sanctified, I could just trust him and none of these things would be an issue.

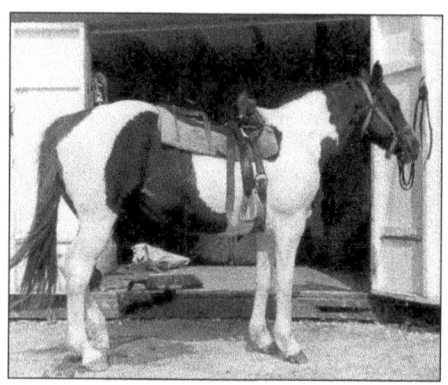
Empty Saddle...Missing Partner

The last 2 years of our marriage was hell. I was still doing a residency in another state, I didn't know what was going on, and he announced (just after I told him I could see light at the end of the tunnel, I was 6 months away from graduation, coming back home, and we could try to start a family which was his heart's desire) that he didn't know if he wanted to be married to me anymore. Some dear friends to this present day, Randy and Fran Rodebaugh, stood with me in my move back to Ohio and shared that my husband had stopped attending church although pretending to still go. He had stopped wearing his wedding ring for 3 years whenever away from me. I had Randy keep my Dad's 22 rifle for me so I would not be able to even be tempted to use it to kill myself.

I was angry at first, then shock and denial followed quickly. I immediately began to reach out to Dr. Dan Tipton for counseling and advice since he was general superintendent of our denomination, and knew both Kathy and me from our early days at Nipgen Camp. When first introduced, he told us that we could call him "Dan," which at age 15, made us feel very important indeed. Dr. Tipton, (Dan), was our go-to person for searching out meaning to life's difficult questions. I read multiple books on saving marriages, tearfully praying every day for at least 1 1/2 to 2 hours. Additionally, I underwent the displeasure of an attending physician for taking too much time off on weekends while I was trying to save my marriage. I couldn't tell *him,* or anyone at work, what was happening! At the same time, I was studying to pass the Medical Board examination.

Although my first husband started coming to marital therapy counseling with me, it didn't last and he didn't want to change anything to make it work. I felt trapped and scared and very alone. When the words "spiritual adultery" were mentioned at a counseling session, I realized that I could initiate a divorce based on Scripture without worrying about it being sin. I also realized that my sister-friend, Kathy, would definitely not be opposed to the idea when she said, "You don't deserve this." Getting the divorce was life-saving for me as I was circling the drain and had contemplated many times how I could commit suicide and still make it to Heaven. I had even posed the question to Dr. Dan by phone who told me that he could see no alternative.

So, the divorce finalized in September of 1996. That same year I was told by the Tiptons that the hospital in the same town where Kathy and I went to Bible College together, was starting a new maternity ward later the following year and, asked if I would be willing to come back to the area? It turned out to be perfect timing! God still had a Divine Plan for my life and my emotional healing began to soar as steps to come back "home" and start a new job took place. I would be close to Kathy! I would be joining the church Kathy and I attended while at the Bible College, and Kathy and I could actually visit in person without the previous distance barrier while I was away at both medical school and in completing my residency.

Despite the chaos in my life, I never forgot my primary calling to be a full time missionary. So, in the summer of 1997, I applied to World Gospel Mission (WGM). They needed an OB/GYN doctor at Tenwek Hospital where I was in 1980. Sounded like it was meant to be! I interviewed and took their Bible History test. One part was whether certain events happened in I & II Samuel, I & II

Kings, or I & II Chronicles. My home Pastor (mentioned earlier – A.B. Maloy, Jr. whom we always affectionately called "Junior"), preached a lot about various stories in those books, so I did very well. They told me that they would not actually ever tell me my score because it was so high, I beat out members on their own Board of Trustees, and that would be embarrassing. One examiner exclaimed, "Wow, a doctor who also knows her Bible!" God gave me this ability and I thank Him for it.

The WGM interview went well, but I was beginning to wonder if I had had enough time for emotional healing to take place in my own life such that I could give my all to becoming a missionary doctor. I shared this concern with a pastor, Rev. Don Spurgeon, who alerted Dr. Dan Tipton. Dr. Dan met with me about the WGM position and I remember he said, "You are afraid they'll say no, and you are afraid they will say yes." He was right and I agreed with his observation! I'm convinced that he communicated with Dr. Tom Hermiz, President of WGM, and Tom told me that they would consider letting me go to the mission field, but that I had to have proof from both my Neurosurgeon and my Urologist that I had a medical release to do it. So, WGM didn't say yes, nor did they say no. It gently let me off the hook. My Neurosurgeon hesitated and my Urologist advised against it cautiously since my condition could worsen, and being in a third world country could be fatal without the medical facilities available in the USA.

My precious husband, Dr. David Miller, helped me reframe my calling. David reasoned with me that while God wasn't changing His <u>calling</u> on my life, He might be changing the <u>mission</u> <u>field</u> of service. Circleville, Ohio was to be my mission field. Circleville was Jerusalem to me. Once again, if I had not felt God's calling so strongly on my life to pursue foreign missions (what I understood as a child), then I likely would have never made it but given up when times became really tough.

Chapter 10
Multiple Surgeries & Treatments

Throughout my life, I have undergone multiple urinary procedures including dilation and multiple sling procedures of various types – every time a new type became available, they would try it on me. We tried combinations of surgeries, collagen injections, and many different trials of anti-spasmotic medications throughout my teen and young adult years. These meds were dehydrating agents and caused my parotid gland to be chronically and severely scarred and narrowed so that I had to discontinue them. The doctor said they would have led to cancer of the parotid gland had I continued the drugs. These drugs also made my mouth terribly dry and caused me to drink more water which, in turn, led to more problems with the bladder spasm ordeals.

The dehydrating drugs also contributed to severe constipation, and I already had a paralyzed colon with a muscle control factor of 1 on a scale of 1 to 4. This meant that I had precious little control of that area as well, and this has slowly worsened over the years. A couple of years ago I consulted with a colorectal surgeon who did not want to try and correct this problem with a surgery to tighten the sphincter since my muscle control factor, as mentioned, is only a 1 and any type of surgery could weaken that further. So, regulation is an ongoing daily challenge for me now. One of the reasons I retired at 60 years of age was to be able to be at home more, close to the bathroom, as I need to constantly balance how many stool softeners and mild laxatives to take.

I also have had 4 spinal cord surgeries to try and remove the fatty tumor at the base of the spine. It was not malignant, but nearly impossible to remove until laser surgery became possible. I was 35 years old, working with Dr. Ed Ricaurte at the time, when I got an appointment with a pediatric neurosurgeon. This was necessary because although an adult, I had a pediatric problem. Very few people with my condition have made it to adulthood. The urinary control, actually the lack thereof, had increased to the point of having to wear a foley catheter attached to a leg bag to perform surgeries that lasted more than an hour. Then, control became nonexistent. I was constantly leaking.

Dr. Michael Healy, the only pediatric neurosurgeon in that city, graciously took me as a patient and insisted that I absolutely needed surgery the very next day on an emergent basis. He told me that once the central nervous system is involved to that degree, it is impossible to recover function and could become worse. A slight inconvenience was that he was leaving the following day after my surgery for a week in the Cayman Islands and I would be turned over to a neurosurgeon who only did adult neurosurgery and had never seen this kind of issue. So, this was during the time of my marital separation - and my husband never came in once to see me. Mom came up to stay at the hospital with me and was ok for a few days until I let a nurse wash my hair. Mom became livid, stating that since I didn't need her anymore, she would go home, and then left.

I was confined to bedrest, lying flat because I had developed a spinal fluid leak. As a surgeon, I knew all too well the risks of this condition, including death. I called Kathy to tell her and confide in my best friend. I really didn't expect her response to me; she called her husband, Tim, and they both rearranged their entire work schedules and came up to take care of me. Kathy told me she just said, "Tim, Joy needs me!" And, they did it. They visited me at the hospital and stayed at my apartment where they took care of my American Eskimo, "Snowball." Kathy told me that Snowball stayed on my bed and growled if

"HOLD ON, *My Child!*"

they moved at all, so they took the spare bedroom and slept on just a mattress with box springs for several nights until Mom came back to stay with me again.

Snowball...faithful loyalty

"Snowball" was there for me when my husband left home for the last time. She had always loved him and had spent many an evening on his lap, but when he told me good-bye and called to her to say the same thing, that dog would not look at him. She was lying down turned away from him, and did not move, her eyes fixed on me. He said, "Fine, I won't say goodbye!" and left. I will always believe that dog sensed that something was terribly wrong and that I desperately needed her to stay with me.

Back to my story about the spinal cord surgery, during the week of lying flat, I went through a major spiritual warfare. It seemed very, very dark indeed. I had a potentially life-threatening spinal fluid leak, my husband was gone, Mom had deserted me, and I might not ever be able to return to work with Dr. Ricaurte. I was praying in desperation one night when I had a dream or vision of some sort. I was in the most foul-smelling area of filth and debris that

I have ever experienced. There were wooden bridges that I was trying to get over, but couldn't because the filth made them too slippery. I traveled all around this chain-linked fenced-in compound-of-sorts to try and find a way of escape. There was no way out; I thought it was hell. I finally made it to the top of a raised bridge, the stench of the filth being nearly overwhelming, when I saw a demon determined to impale me with some object.

In that second, after hours and hours of futilely wandering around trying to find a way of escape, a huge angel with white wings came down from above, picked me up, carried me over the chain-linked fence, and set me in a beautiful green pasture. I saw the huge black demon standing beside my hospital bed at 3:30 AM, rebuked it in Jesus' name, and it immediately left. The Holy Spirit whispered to me "It's all over." I KNEW what that meant instantaneously. It <u>didn't</u> mean that I was instantly healed. It meant that any surgery I had from then on, and whatever I went through, would be for my <u>healing</u> and not my destruction.

I slept for 6 straight hours, wonderful, peaceful, solid sleep and woke up refreshed. I also knew in my heart that I could get up and that it would be okay to walk to the bathroom to get cleaned up by myself. I carefully did just that without asking; I knew my nurse would never allow it. The spinal fluid leak just underneath my skin had become the size of a football. When the doctor came by on rounds to tell me that my pediatric neurosurgeon would be back the next day to examine the leak, I smiled and told him that I was much better. I was able to get up and move about without any worsening of the problem and had no spinal headache at all. He was so stunned that he couldn't say anything. He just left speechless.

Dr. Tipton came up to visit as well as Dr. David Lattimer, our General Missionary Superintendent. I shared that after my dream, I didn't feel ecstatic at all, heard no bells, saw no heavenly choirs. Dr. Tipton said, "You felt neutral." That was true – peaceful, calm, and neutral. I had complete resolution that all would be okay. When my own neurosurgeon returned from the Cayman Islands, he took me back to surgery. I had called Dr. Tipton's and Dr. Lattimer's office and all the staff there stopped whatever they were doing at noon, and had a special prayer meeting for me. The leak was fixed and I did not need a drain which would have been a major potential for developing meningitis. When I woke up from the surgery I could report to them, "No leak, no drain, home tomorrow!"

The tumor was completely removed and, for a while, my urinary symptoms improved. I returned to work with my senior partner, Dr. Ed Ricaurte, who informed me that a local hospital, Parkview, was closing and suggested I ask them to donate equipment to Tenwek Hospital. We figured I could ask and that the worst they could do was give an answer of "no". I met with the CEO who immediately said, "Yes"! Dr. Richard & Betty Morse, missionaries to Tenwek Hospital, were in the states on furlough and met with me to go through the closed hospital determining what could be used. We tagged over $500,000 worth of beds, tables, X-ray equipment, lab equipment, and virtually everything in the hospital because we were the first to ask. It was going to cost over $7,000 to have it shipped to WGM headquarters in Marion, IN. My jaw must have dropped when the CEO ordered the transport via 3 extra-large semi-trucks and volunteered to cover the cost in its entirety! I wanted to give him publicity for being so extremely generous but he declined saying, "Just take the gift and run with it." It helped fill up 3 warehouses at WGM and all of it eventually arrived at Tenwek hospital via governmental aircraft which was supplied at no cost.

Chapter 11
MY TESTIMONY

I wrote a testimony in 1999 describing some things I endured from late 1994 on. It was given at Circleville Jefferson (later Crossroads) church. Some of the following may be repetitious, but I have decided to include the full testimony. A large portion of it was printed in *Today's Christian Doctor* magazine entitling my testimony as **"Even When God is Silent."**

> *Between 1994 and 1996, I had lost literally everything of major importance in my life. At that time, I was married to a husband who had decided to turn away from God, the Faith, and what we had believed in. He went heavily into alcoholism and pornography. At times, I thought that even my life might be in danger.*

Financial difficulties ensued after the divorce. As a result, I lost my home and a pet horse. I also found out shortly thereafter that my childhood best friend, Jody, had been diagnosed with colon cancer. She died nine weeks later. I tried multiple times to pray with her during that time and was met with resistance. Her husband was not comforting as he told me that she said right before she died that she was afraid to die.

I felt like a total failure in absolutely every aspect of my life. I could not understand why any of this was happening. I was a Child of God, I had gone to Bible College, I was raised in a fundamental Bible-believing church, and, I was planning to become a full-time foreign missionary!

I really truly felt like I lived with Job through the book of Job. In the first chapter when he lost everything – even his spouse turned on him, and through the middle part – the questioning and doubts that led to months of praying. I prayed to God every night for hours. I would cry, earnestly pray, and search the Scriptures, yet did not hear from Heaven. God chose to be silent during that time. For 18 grueling months I did not get any comfort from the Scriptures about my situation. My prayers seemed to go unanswered. I did not sense any blessings from God. I was very close to despair.

I could relate to Job where he says (paraphrase) "God, I look in front of me and You are not there…I look behind me and can't find You…I look on my right hand and on my left hand and I can't see You." However, then his faith begins to rise and Job says, (paraphrase) "God, even though I don't know where You are, You know where I am! And when You have tried me, I shall come forth as gold." (Job 23: 8-10). Job had also said, "I know that my Redeemer lives!" (Job 19:25).

I determined in my heart that no matter what happened, if I never heard from Heaven again, if I never got any comfort out of the Scriptures, if I never felt another blessing of God, I would stand on my experiences of salvation and sanctification to the end.

Just like Job, I began to have some severe physical problems. I had been born with a spinal cord tumor that started to cause significant physical impairment. The tumor was benign, but it was still causing major physical compromise and I was going to be faced with three major surgeries in order to try and help correct the problems.

I remember in January of 1997, in the hospital during recovery of the first major surgery, God came to me, finally, and whispered, "It's all over." I knew that He meant the months of suffering were over…it was in the past…healing was coming. I knew that the future surgeries would be for my healing and not my destruction. I would once again experience the blessings of God. Physical healing began, gradually, and World Gospel Mission gave approval for short-term mission trips.

Also, during the hospital stay, God began to give me a spiritual revival and renewal. Once again I was able to glean things from the Word of God that meant something special to my life. I felt that my prayers were being answered. Financial healing came as God began to reverse the present situation. So, with the physical, spiritual, and financial healing, also, obviously, emotional healing began to come. I passed my OB/GYN oral board exam and accepted an offer from a hospital close to my home town. They were opening up a brand new maternity ward and this enabled me to return to the same town where I *had attended Bible College. I returned to the same wonderful church that I attended during Bible College years, entered fellowship with brothers and sisters that I hadn't seen in 16 years, and my support system grew by leaps and bounds. But, the best was yet to come.*

David (left) with Joy and Dr. Dan Tipton (right)

In 1998, I began to date Dr. David Miller. The loss of a spouse creates a void that nothing else can fill and God brought Dr. Miller into my life. We began dating and in January of 1999, we married. Dr. Dan Tipton performed the ceremony.

In David, God provided me with a Christian man full of utmost integrity that I can trust. He loves me, supports me, and takes care of me. He proves to me that I'm important to him, and he's proud of me. David is the best gift that God has ever given to me, second only to salvation and sanctification. David has provided me once again with a safe beautiful home and then to *add icing on the cake, just a little over a week ago, he got me a horse!*

So, although I really felt like I could identify with Job in the first chapter and all through the book, even in the last chapter I can now identify with Job. God restored all things to Job. The Bible says that the latter part of Job's life was better than the first. And I can say "Praise the Lord…that is me…that's where I'm living now!" God has restored all things to me and the quality is better than I've ever had before. I want to thank God for all these blessings! I'm thankful people were praying for me, God was faithful, and He brought me through! I'm glad that I held on through the long night; through the deep tunnel when it seemed like the light at the end of the tunnel went out. I'm so thankful that I held on! Blessings, Hope, and Joy comes in the morning if we hold fast, remain true, pure, and faithful to Him…He <u>will</u> reward us!

Following my testimony, I asked Worship Leader, Rev. Gary Ingo, to sing a song written by Gloria & Bill Gaither, entitled "Joy Comes In The Morning." The lyrics to that song follow:

Verse:
If you've knelt beside the rubble of an aching, broken heart;
When the things you gave your life to fell apart,
You're not the first to be acquainted with sorrow, grief, or pain.
But the Master promised sunshine after rain.

Verse:
Now to invest your seed of trust in God in mountains you can't move;
You have risked your life on things you cannot prove
Just to give the things you cannot keep for what you cannot lose
That's the way to find the joy God has for you!

Chorus:
Hold on, my child!
Joy comes in the morning!
Weeping only lasts for the night.
Hold on my child!
Joy comes in the morning
For the darkest hour means dawn is just in sight.

Chapter 12
GOD'S ENABLING GRACE

As for my office practice, my prayers were consistently to the tune of no matter where patients stood spiritually with God upon entering my doors, I prayed that they would be closer to God upon leaving. I prayed before performing all my surgeries and procedures. I wanted most of all to have God with me in the operating room or delivery room guiding my hands and speaking wisdom and knowledge to my heart. Many times my patients and even staff would ask me to pray about a concern or issue. I felt deeply honored by their request; and would pray with them in my office or in the exam rooms. While practicing, I would start each day with

Joy Shields, MD, OBGYN & Surgeon

prayer before beginning any routine. I also prayed for my husband's patients in his psychology practice. I still pray every day, multiple times every day, and daily read Scripture. It is the best way to live.

Chapter 13

GOD BROUGHT SURGICAL HEALING TO THE SURGEON

Several years later, in March 2008, at 47 years old, I was finally able to convince a Gyn-urologist at the Cleveland Clinic to consider an Indiana Pouch procedure for me. It would include removal of my entire bladder and urethra, my right colon converted into a new bladder with conduit to the right lower quadrant of my abdomen that I could catheterize every 2 to 3 hours, the rest of my intestines sewed back together inside making it one again with normal physiological outlet, and a total hysterectomy as I suffered monthly with pain from endometriosis and a fibroid uterus. These last issues were likely why I was never able to get pregnant. <u>I knew</u> this Indiana pouch procedure would <u>*work*</u> and give me significantly improved freedom! I believed that without even a tiny doubt – I was convinced by faith that God was going to heal me in a significant way with this extensive surgery.

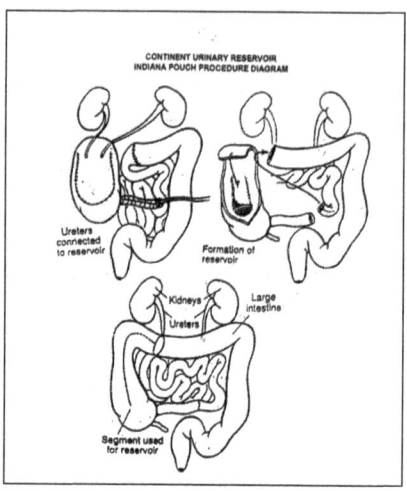

Diagram of Indiana Pouch Procedure

This was predicted to be an 8 hour surgery with 2 specialized surgeons but they finished in 5 1/2 hours. Rev. Lonnie Potts and missionary friends Rev. Ken & Carol Mossor each drove to Cleveland to be with David during the surgery and drove back home in a blinding snowstorm that resulted in 2 feet of snow. I was scheduled to be in the ICU for several hours but was admitted instead to a regular floor. David says even now that I had enough tubes coming out of so many areas of my body, that it was enough to plumb a small building!

I was in Cleveland Clinic for a week, went home, but 4 weeks later needed admitted into a hospital in my home town for IV antibiotics because I developed bilateral pyelonephritis (severe infection in both kidneys). My catheter got clogged in my conduit and my newly formed bladder from my right colon almost exploded before the problem was figured out. At about 3:30 AM the following day after admission, I noticed my gown in front was very wet with urine. I rang for the nurse and posed the question wondering if something was wrong with my catheter. He offered to bring me a new one and once inserted, an additional 1700 ml of fluid was produced. So...my new bladder was actually trying to hold 2 liters! This had caused excruciating pain like a gigantic colonic cramp. David feared that I was going to die, and my admitting doctors were planning on life-flighting me by helicopter back up to Cleveland Clinic in just a few hours for emergency surgery.

When I called David at 4:00 AM, he was wonderfully shocked to hear me exclaiming, "Do you believe in miracles? I'm OK! No need to rush in to see me and no need to travel to Cleveland Clinic – I am fine!" And, I was. No other significant issues like that have ever occurred since that time. It caused us to love and appreciate each other even more than we already did, which was a ton. In the interim from 1999 – 2008, we had sold all 3 of our horses and moved closer to the hospital (within 5 miles into a community in which no livestock was allowed) since I was getting called in for OB matters nearly every day and night. Sometimes multiple times, including over the weekends. I had no time to take care of one horse, much less 2 or 3.

As David sat by my side in that hospital, when he thought I was going to die, he told me later that all he could think of was that I wanted horses so badly and didn't have one. He resolved to do whatever it took to help me get another one. He now jokes by saying he made the mistake of telling me his resolve and that I kept him to his word.

Joy with "Rowdy"

Chapter 14
FINAL YEARS OF PRACTICE

My Dad was to turn 80 on May 18th of this same year, 2008. I did not tell him about my surgery because he had had several strokes and I knew it would be too hard on him. We visited with him on Wednesday night prior to his Sunday birthday. At that time, he told me that he wanted to let me know that if he didn't live a day past 80, that it would be ok with him. I had hugged and kissed him but felt impressed to hug him again. I was so glad I did because we got a call Saturday night that he had gotten choked on a piece of chicken and likely suffered a massive stroke. He never recovered;

Dr. Joy Shields-Miller

and, therefore did not live a day past his 80th birthday. He is now in Heaven with my sister, Kathy, waiting for me.

At the end of that year, 2008, I decided to only do GYN so I stopped all the OB 24/7 on-call. That was a relief but soon got boring so I prayed for God to give me something else to do. Little did I know that a cardiovascular surgeon had put forth a proposal to my hospital to train someone to do procedures for varicose veins. Being a surgeon, I was a perfect fit and was asked to do this just 2 weeks after I had prayed! That was fun and successful and soon I was approached to go full scale by Wendy Elliott, COO, to oversee and help treat arterial and vein problems in the wound clinic. This occurred in 2015 and toward the end of that year, I became the wound and hyperbaric oxygen clinics' Medical Director. This continued until I retired January 4, 2021, at the age of 60 for reasons stated earlier and because David retired in December of 2020. We wanted to spend more time together.

Regarding David's desire to get me another horse, we started looking for a new place to live. In

Drs. David & Joy Shields-Miller

2013, we found a home on 10 acres, but converted it into two roughly five acre plots and after 5 years, built our dream home in the front part with a building/stable and pasture for a horse in the back yard...just as I always wanted. Following my last surgery in 2008, I was able to play softball and run again with no fear of embarrassing accidents! I know it looks weird, as old as I am, for me to be out on a softball field, but it is like reliving childhood and teen years over again when I try to master the shortstop position. I still have to wear a pad over my conduit's opening to soak up minor leakage, and, one for possible minor stool spillage, but that is a thousand percent more freeing than wearing a full time Foley catheter!

I am certain that our precious grandchildren, and even our kids, have had little to no idea about all of this...until they read my story. ☺ Our kids and grandchildren are the love of our lives and if I was to write about all the immeasurable blessings they each have brought into our lives, it would take another book!

We transferred our membership to a little church, Hedges Chapel, in 2020, the year during the Covid crisis. We are doing what we can to minister to peoples' needs there. We are also praying that God will give us a ministry that we can do together and look forward to more short term mission trips in the South and Southwest United States, when Covid lifts and travel is possible again, as I am able to navigate my handicaps in non-third world areas. In the past, before my major surgery and before my condition became so troubling, David and I went on short term mission trips to Southwest USA, as well as Kenya, Africa (twice), Bolivia, Honduras, and St. Croix. Some of the missionaries we have been privileged to work and share with are: Dr. Ernie Steury, Dr. Richard & Betty Morse, Dr. Eric & Jodi Miller, Dr. Mike Johnson, Dr. Mary Hermiz, Rev. Dan & Peggy Zimmerman, Butch & Leatha Jenkins, Rev. Ken & Carol Mossor, Rev. Mike & Donna Brown, Rev. Tom & Jackie Amlin, Rev. Tim & Sharon Hawk, Kent & Rhonda Harmless, and Rev. Steve & Debbie Cartwright. We treasure these memories, especially me, since a large part of my mission's heart remains in Kenya even now. My precious prayer partner, Leatha Jenkins (missionary to Papua, New Guinea), and I meet regularly for sharing and praying over special requests when she is back in America on furlough.

A final note about my mom--although I was excluded entirely from her Will, and kept locked out of her home by not providing a key for us; she left me a letter to be read after her death. She recently passed at the age of 89. The letter began "Dear Joy," and contained the words, "I love you...and I will be waiting for you to come to Heaven." It was signed "Love, Mother." Perhaps it was the best she could do.

As for my life-long friend, Kathy, to this day we still joke about our kind-of pact made in our early years at

Bible College; that inevitably, she and I would likely finish out our most elderly years (90s – 100s) in a nursing home, together again, as roommates.

Chapter 15
A Multitude of Positive Influences Along the Way

Many people influenced my life in memorable ways, some are mentioned in a major part of my story, but others are listed below:

Mr. Charles Bowman - High School chemistry teacher – encouraged me to become a doctor

Jim & Connie Bowman – Provided me a safe place to stay after my divorce, were camp coordinators par excellence

Churches of Christ in Christian Union Missionaries, Pastors, & Evangelists

Crossroads' CATS Sunday School Class – engaged in deep spiritual discussions and had "Second Sunday" fellowships – not necessarily on the second Sunday

Wendy Elliott – Executive Director and COO of Ohio Health Berger - my champion and cheerleader during both good times and difficult times while I was a physician

Rev. Wayland & June Hamlin – my first camp coordinators, Wayland was my pitcher and I was his shortstop in all softball games

Hedges Chapel friends – newly met but cherished fellowships during Covid crisis

Dr. & Mrs Tom Hermiz – President of World Gospel Mission and dear friends

Dr. Mary Hermiz – Godly missionary lady who started the Tenwek Hospital School of Nursing. She is fun-loving and always a delight. Truly an inspiration for missions to all who know her

Rev. Wayne & Jean Hiles – provided huge laughs and the home getaway for Kathy and me

Rev. A.B. & Marjorie Maloy - early childhood to young adult years' Pastor

Bill & Jane Marietta - Sunday School teachers who provided the best games and laughter at Youth parties

Rev. Melvin & Betty Maxwell – President of Circleville Bible College (CBC), told me that he could tell, when I was only 8 years old, by looking in my eyes that I was a straight "A" student and would be coming to CBC

Dr. & Mrs. David Lattimer - Spiritual giants and missionary leaders

Rev. L.B. & Ruth Miller – David's parents, my Godly in-laws

Orange Blossom Fellowship – Retreat home in Florida for David and me. Extraordinary friends met there.

Rev. Steve & Debbie Palmer – current pastoral team who provide unwavering support and love to us and our little church – Hedges Chapel

Dr. Nelson & Barbara Perdue – Spiritual guidance and insight

Dr. & Mrs. Jim Pollard - Dean of Students at Circleville Bible College, now Ohio Christian University – was my boss and friend when I was secretary

Rev. Lonnie Potts – pastor of Circleville Crossroads Church when I returned "home" and our pastor for many years while at Crossroads Church

Dr. Ed Ricaurte – Senior partner in OB/GYN and the best partner ever

Shields' family relatives – aunts, uncles, cousins – tight knit group

Miss Alyce Smith - High School Spanish teacher – told me I should become a doctor because I would be <u>honest</u> with patient's families

Rev. Don & Aggie Spurgeon - Pastor & Missionaries to Dominican Republic

Dr. Eugene and Faye Stowe – were an extra set of "parents" to David and me

Dr. Stan Toler – expounder of the faith and values to young and old

Dr. Robert A. Welch – Senior Perinatologist, Residency Director, research mentor, and hero

Ruth Wence – elderly lady who was my supporter and encourager in elementary and high school years – answered a multitude of questions about the Bible and life in general

Rev. Norman & Nancy Wilson – Another set of Godly "parents" to us

To all these and others, I owe a debt of gratitude.

www.ingramcontent.com/pod-product-compliance
Ingram Content Group UK Ltd.
Pitfield, Milton Keynes, MK11 3LW, UK
UKHW022216230426
12048UKWH00016BA/882